Franklin D. Roosevelt

by Erin Edison

Consulting Editor: Gail Saunders-Smith, PhD

Consultant:
Sheila Blackford
Librarian, Scripps Library
Managing Editor, *American President*
Miller Center, University of Virginia

CAPSTONE PRESS
a capstone imprint

Pebble Plus is published by Capstone Press,
1710 Roe Crest Drive, North Mankato, Minnesota 56003.
www.capstonepub.com

Library of Congress Cataloging-in-Publication Data
Edison, Erin.
  Franklin D. Roosevelt / by Erin Edison.
    p. cm.—(Pebble plus. Presidential biographies)
  Includes bibliographical references and index.
  Summary: "Simple text and full-color photographs describe the life of Franklin D. Roosevelt"—Provided by publisher.
  ISBN 978-1-4296-8736-2 (library binding)
  ISBN 978-1-62065-317-3 (ebook PDF)
  1. Roosevelt, Franklin D. (Franklin Delano), 1882–1945—Juvenile literature. 2. Presidents—United States—
Biography—Juvenile literature. I. Title.
  E807.E35 2013
  973.917092—dc23
  [B]   2011049858

Editorial Credits
Erika L. Shores, editor; Sarah Bennett, designer; Wanda Winch, media researcher; Kathy McColley,
    production specialist

Photo Credits
Corbis: Bettmann, 13, Oscar White, cover; The Franklin D. Roosevelt Presidential Library, 5, 7, 9, 21; Library of
Congress: Prints and Photographs Division, 1, 11, 15, 17; National Archives and Records Administration, 19

Note to Parents and Teachers

The Presidential Biographies series supports national history standards related to people and
culture. This book describes and illustrates the life of Franklin D. Roosevelt. The images
support early readers in understanding the text. The repetition of words and phrases helps early
readers learn new words. This book also introduces early readers to subject-specific vocabulary
words, which are defined in the Glossary section. Early readers may need assistance to read
some words and to use the Table of Contents, Glossary, Read More, Internet Sites, and Index
sections of the book.

Printed in the United States of America in North Mankato, Minnesota.
042012   006682CGF12

Table of Contents

Early Years

Franklin Delano Roosevelt led

the United States through

a difficult time in history.

The future president was born

January 30, 1882, in New York.

His family was rich. Nannies and

tutors cared for and taught Franklin.

born in
New York

1882

Young Franklin in 1888

In 1896 Franklin attended

a private school in Massachusetts.

There, he was taught to help others,

especially the poor. Franklin

graduated from Harvard

University in 1903. He later

attended Columbia Law School.

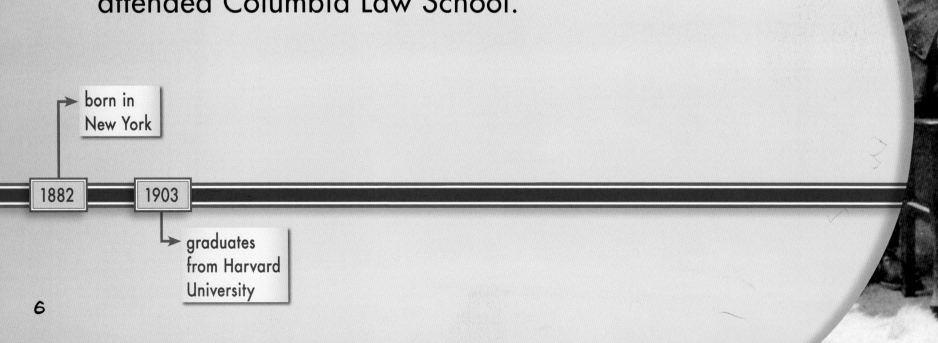

born in
New York

1882

1903

graduates
from Harvard
University

THE
HARVARD CRIMSON

There will be a Meeting of the Editors
the Sanctum at 6.45 P. M.

Franklin (front row, center) at Harvard

Young Adult

Franklin married Eleanor Roosevelt
in 1905. They were distant cousins.
Franklin and Eleanor had
one daughter and five sons.
One son died as a baby.
The couple shared a belief
in helping people.

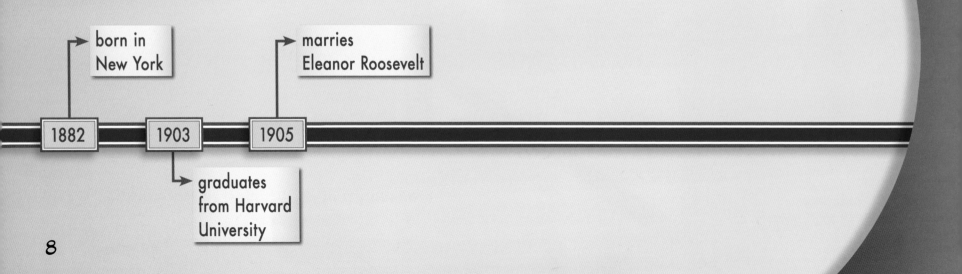

born in
New York

marries
Eleanor Roosevelt

1882   1903   1905

graduates
from Harvard
University

Franklin, Eleanor (center) and their family in 1919

Franklin was elected to
the New York State Senate
in 1910. He later worked
as the assistant secretary of
the U.S. Navy. In 1928 he was
elected governor of New York.

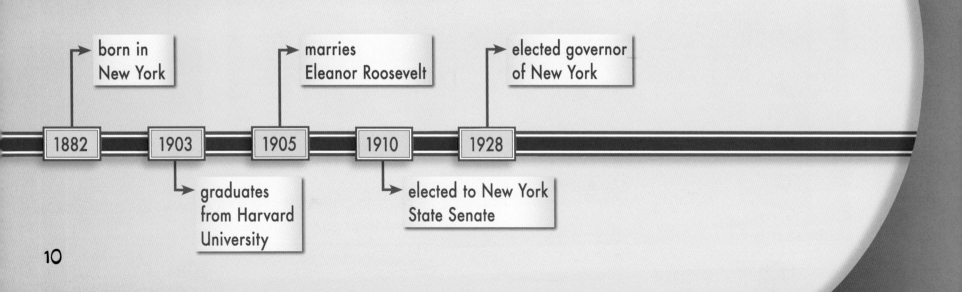

| born in New York | | marries Eleanor Roosevelt | | elected governor of New York |

| 1882 | 1903 | 1905 | 1910 | 1928 |

graduates from Harvard University

elected to New York State Senate

Franklin speaking in New York in 1920

In 1921 Franklin became sick
with polio. He couldn't walk
without help.
He walked with crutches
or had someone help him.
He later used a wheelchair.

born in
New York

marries
Eleanor Roosevelt

elected governor
of New York

1882   1903   1905   1910   1928

graduates
from Harvard
University

elected to New York
State Senate

President Roosevelt

Franklin became the 32nd
U.S. president in 1933. At the time,
many Americans did not have
jobs, food, or homes. This period
is called the Great Depression.
Franklin had to find ways
to fix the country's problems.

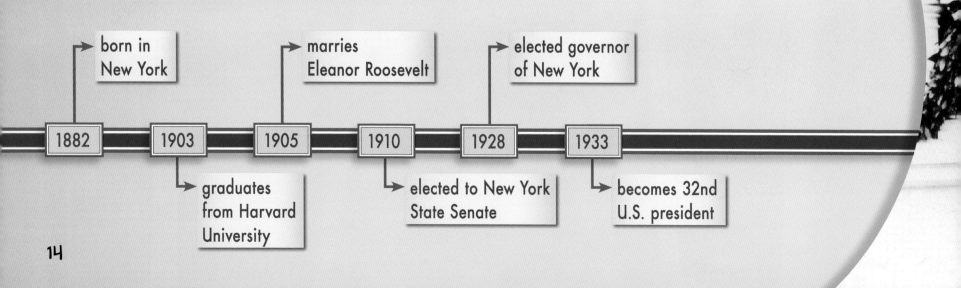

born in
New York

marries
Eleanor Roosevelt

elected governor
of New York

| 1882 | 1903 | 1905 | 1910 | 1928 | 1933 |

graduates
from Harvard
University

elected to New York
State Senate

becomes 32nd
U.S. president

Working with Congress,

Franklin created programs

and jobs to help Americans.

He called these plans

the "New Deal." Franklin spoke

to Americans about his plans

during radio speeches.

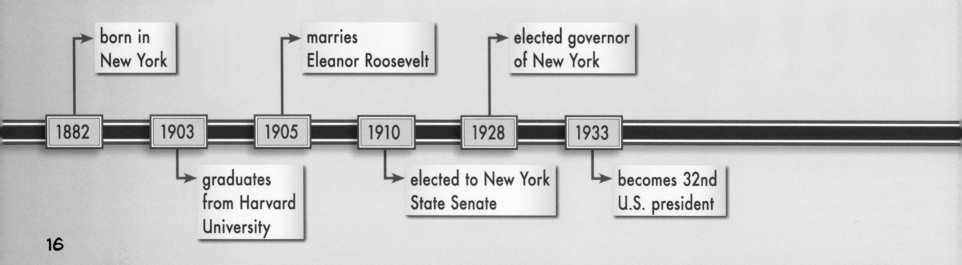

born in
New York

marries
Eleanor Roosevelt

elected governor
of New York

1882   1903   1905   1910   1928   1933

graduates
from Harvard
University

elected to New York
State Senate

becomes 32nd
U.S. president

World War II (1939–1945)

started in 1939. Two years later,

the United States joined the war.

Franklin and other Americans

worked hard to win the war.

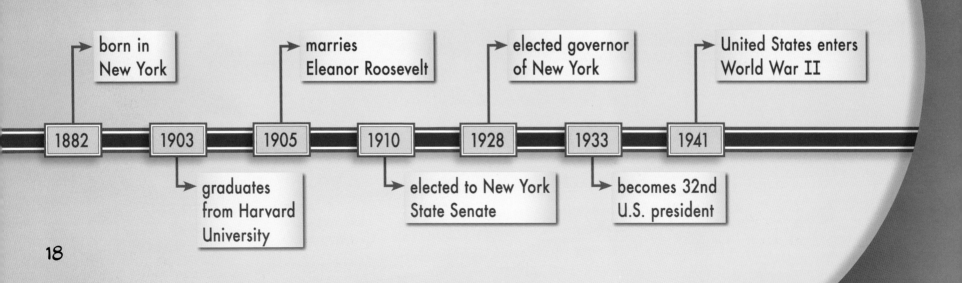

born in
New York

marries
Eleanor Roosevelt

elected governor
of New York

United States enters
World War II

| 1882 | 1903 | 1905 | 1910 | 1928 | 1933 | 1941 |

graduates
from Harvard
University

elected to New York
State Senate

becomes 32nd
U.S. president

Franklin signing Declaration of War in 1941

Remembering Roosevelt

Franklin was elected president four times. No other president has served as many terms in office. In 1945 Franklin died suddenly. People remember him as a strong leader and a great president.

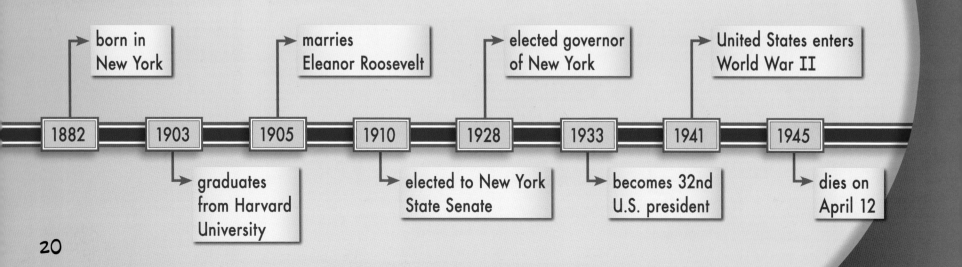

born in New York		**marries Eleanor Roosevelt**		**elected governor of New York**		**United States enters World War II**	
1882	1903	1905	1910	1928	1933	1941	1945
	graduates from Harvard University		**elected to New York State Senate**		**becomes 32nd U.S. president**		**dies on April 12**

Glossary

Congress—the elected government body of the United States that makes laws

elect—to choose someone as a leader by voting

Great Depression—a period of hard times, when there were few jobs in the United States, and most people had little money or food; it lasted throughout the 1930s and ended with America's entry into World War II

nanny—someone who is trained to take care of young children in the children's homes

polio—a disease that attacks a person's nerves, spinal cord, and brain

tutor—a teacher who gives lessons to only one student or a small group of students

World War II—a war in which the United States, France, Great Britain, the Soviet Union and other countries defeated Germany, Italy, and Japan

Read More

Gosman, Gillian. *Franklin D. Roosevelt.* Life Stories. New York: PowerKids Press, 2011.

Krull, Kathleen. *A Boy Named FDR: How Franklin D. Roosevelt Grew Up to Change America.* New York: Alfred A. Knopf, 2011.

Lee, Sally. *Eleanor Roosevelt.* First Ladies. Mankato, Minn.: Capstone Press, 2011.

Internet Sites

FactHound offers a safe, fun way to find Internet sites related to this book. All of the sites on FactHound have been researched by our staff.

Here's all you do:

Visit *www.facthound.com*

Type in this code: 9781429687362

 Super-cool stuff! Check out projects, games and lots more at **www.capstonekids.com**

Index

Word Count: 282

Grade: 1

Early-Intervention Level: 21